CHANGE
Beyond The Pain

TRANSFORMATION IS WITHIN YOUR REACH

WORKBOOK

Your Life Is Worth Examining!

MONIFA ROBINSON GROOVER

CHANGE
Beyond The Pain

WORKBOOK

CHANGE
Beyond The Pain

TRANSFORMATION IS WITHIN YOUR REACH

WORKBOOK

YOUR LIFE IS WORTH EXAMINING!

MONIFA ROBINSON GROOVER

Change Beyond The Pain…Transformation is Within Your Reach Workbook…Your Life is Worth Examining

Copyright © 2013 by Monifa Robinson Groover
Published by Vision Publishing House, LLC
Savannah, Georgia 31420
www.visionpublishinghouse.com

ISBN: 978-0-9836776-2-8
eBook ISBN: 978-0-9836776-3-5

Final Editing: www.egen.co
Cover Design: www.egen.co
Book Layout: www.egen.co

Follow us on Twitter: @WYRInspires
Follow us on Facebook: Within Your Reach

All rights reserved. No part of the material protected by this copyright notice may be reproduced or utilized in any form or by any means, electronic, mechanically, digitally, photocopying, or recording without the written consent/license of the publisher. For permission requests, write to the publisher, addressed "Attention Permissions Coordinator", at the address below.
Vision Publishing House, LLC
P.O. Box 60393
Savannah, GA 31420
www.visionpublishinghouse.com

All Scripture quotations, unless otherwise indicated, are from the King James Version of the Bible. All definitions quoted, unless otherwise indicated, are from an online resource, www.dictionary.com.

Scripture quotations marked "NIV" are taken from *The Holy Bible, New International Version,* © 1973, 1984, 2011 by International Bible Society, used by permission of Zondervan Publishing House.

Published in the United States of America

Contents

Purpose	01
Introduction	05
Chapter 1 – Surrender *It is time to move beyond accepting change to embracing transformation*	11
Chapter 2 – God's Perfect Will *My thoughts are not your thoughts, Nor are my ways your ways*	17
Chapter 3 – God's Perfect Timing *Rest in the Lord and wait patiently for Him*	25
Chapter 4 – All For His Glory…It's Not About Me *Know your role in the Kingdom of God*	37
Chapter 5 – The Power and Purpose of Pain *All things work together for good to them that love God, to them who are the called according to his purpose*	41
Chapter 6 – Faith…But First You MUST Believe! *Faith doesn't ask questions, it simply follows instructions*	47
Chapter 7 – Transformation…It's An Inside Job! *Drilling…Blasting…Refining*	53
Chapter 8 – Transformation is Within Your Reach *Promotion Attained in the Heat of Night*	57

Purpose

Whether you go through this workbook on your own or with a group of people, this workbook is designed to provide you with a very personal experience. It is designed to encourage you to move toward having a more intimate relationship with Christ. This workbook is intended for those who are ready to do the work it takes in order to establish and grow their relationship with Jesus Christ. It is an extension of the book, *Change Beyond The Pain*. If you are willing and ready to do the work, it will help you move forward in your spiritual walk.

In order to move beyond the realm of Change and into the territory of Transformation it is vitally important that one seek truth. Truth is where true healing begins. Most people say they want the truth but I am convinced that once *truth* is presented, reservation sets in, even if only for a moment. This reservation is often due to shock, denial, disbelief, anger and offense, just to name a few. It is my belief that most people don't understand how deep the truth can cut; neither do they understand the magnitude to which it can heal. The reality is that oftentimes truth hurts before it heals.

Most people say they want to heal their emotional wounds and that they are willing to do it at any cost. But the cost is honesty. We must first be willing to acknowledge our vulnerabilities. We must stare our inconsistencies in the face. This is the only way to move past them. Most of us have difficulty doing this because the pain of looking at our own inconsistencies is much too great. The pain we have experienced in life is too much to bear. However, no one ever said we had to confront all of our issues at one time; that would be overwhelming. But the work must begin somewhere. We must realize that healing will indeed come, but only after truth and honesty have taken their rightful place.

How can a patient expect the doctor to fix his broken leg when the only thing he complains about is the pain in his shoulder? The patient must be honest with the doctor and inform him of where the pain actually lies. The same is so with our spiritual healing. We must be honest about the pain that is deeply embedded within us. This pain has caused many to be confused, bound and broken, creating a wedge between them and Christ and thus separating them from the Source who is able to heal all wounds.

Being honest doesn't mean revealing all our faults to the entire world. Neither does the world need to know every demon that has attempted to steal our joy. We must use discretion. Our testimony should always encourage and edify others while glorifying God. Let us also be clear about the fact that honesty begins within. We only display on the outside what is already on the inside. Does our life speak truth or does it speak a lie? Walking in truth and honesty means walking in the Word of God. If we are committed to getting to the next level in Christ, we need to ask ourselves, "Am I walking in truth? Does the Word of God permeate my very being? Am I in the light or am I in darkness?" We must first seek to be honest with ourselves and with God because that is where true healing begins. When we are honest with God we then give Him permission to take us beyond our pain to a place of healing and transformation.

When we walk in truth and honesty, our life then becomes a testimony and a source of healing for others, who then will be able to see that there truly can be *Change Beyond The Pain* and that *Transformation is Within Their Reach*. For them it is no longer some strange mystical phenomenon but has become something real, something tangible and, most importantly, something *doable* that allows them to begin to experience the abundant life Jesus came to give.

Purpose

REFLECTIONS

Throughout this workbook you will find plenty of opportunities for reflection. Within each segment you will find a series of questions designed to help you evaluate where you are in your spiritual walk. The word of God commands us to work out our own salvation (Philippians 2:12). Let me encourage you to take your time and answer these questions truthfully. This may require a level of honesty that you are not accustomed to, but being completely honest with your answers will give you a clearer understanding of where you are and, most importantly, help you determine where you need to go. Remember, transformation is an inside job!

ACTION

The Bible says that we are to be doers of the Word and not hearers only *(James 1:22)*. For this reason you will find a segment at the end of each chapter that will encourage you to take deliberate steps to help you deepen your relationship with Christ. Feel free to repeat these Action Steps more than once and don't hesitate to add or alter a few steps if doing so will assist you in meeting your goals. Just make sure everything is aligned with the Word of God. The key is to keep moving closer and closer toward Jesus Christ.

PRAYER

Communication with God is vitally important. We must constantly seek God's face *(Psalm 27:8)*. Each chapter of this workbook includes a segment that will encourage you to make prayer an active part of your life. You must be open and honest with yourself and with God if you want true healing to take place. Prayer can take place anytime and anywhere. Whether you pray aloud or silently within the innermost parts of your heart, don't ever shut God out. He cares.

It is my hope that this workbook will encourage you and push you beyond your pain so that transformation can become evident in your life. Regardless of where you are in your spiritual walk, I pray blessings, healing, deliverance and wholeness over your life, in Jesus' name.

Introduction

Change Beyond The Pain

Golden Nugget:
> "*the God of our Lord Jesus Christ, the Father of glory, may give unto you the spirit of wisdom and revelation in the knowledge of him: the eyes of your understanding being enlightened; that ye may know what is the hope of his calling, and what the riches of the glory of his inheritance in the saints, and what is the exceeding greatness of his power to us-ward who believe…*" (Ephesians 1:17-19)

There are so many things that hold us captive and keep us from moving forward. Life has a way of stagnating us if we allow it. If we are not careful, we will blame our circumstances and others and never move beyond our pain. Part of moving beyond our pain requires us to take responsibility for our part in the matter.

Taking responsibility is not only about making a verbal declaration about our wrongdoing. It is about getting off the wrong path and pursing the right thing; pursuing greatness; pursuing destiny. But we have to put in the work and that means, first of all, being honest about who we are and what we have done. Only then can we begin to move forward in the right direction.

Cycles…Predictability…Consistency…Regularity…these are just a few things humans crave. Most people never transition to the next level in their lives because they either don't want to change badly enough or are unwilling to do what needs to be done in order for that change to occur.

Going to the next level will ALWAYS require us to move farther, push harder, persevere longer, and dig deeper. Most people sincerely believe they are ready for this, but the true test of our readiness comes when it is actually time to push harder, persevere longer, and dig deeper.

Reflections:

Have you had any life-altering events which caused you to make positive changes in your thinking and in your behavior for a short period of time, only to revert back to your old ways soon after the crisis went away?

a. If so, what was the situation?

_____
_____
_____
_____
_____
_____
_____

b. What caused you to revert back to your old habits?

_____
_____
_____
_____
_____
_____
_____

Introduction

What cycles in your life need to be broken? (Be Specific)

_____
_____
_____
_____
_____
_____
_____
_____
_____
_____
_____
_____

How are these cycles keeping you from transitioning to the next level?

_____
_____
_____
_____
_____
_____
_____
_____
_____
_____
_____
_____
_____

What does the word *Transformation* mean to you?

_____
_____
_____
_____
_____
_____
_____
_____
_____
_____
_____
_____
_____
_____

What has to take place in order for *your* transformation process to begin?

_____
_____
_____
_____
_____
_____
_____
_____
_____
_____
_____
_____
_____
_____

Introduction

Action:

Name one thing you will do differently that shows you are taking responsibility.

_____
_____
_____

Prayer:

Lord, first I want to give thanks and praise to Your holy and righteous name. I thank You in advance for the knowledge, understanding and wisdom You will impart into me as I embark upon my spiritual journey. I ask that You open my spiritual ears so that I may clearly hear the call You have placed on my life. I ask that You open my spiritual eyes that I may clearly see the spiritual things You will reveal to me. I ask that You open my heart so that I may receive Your Word with gladness. Once you have revealed Yourself to me, I ask that You also give me the courage and strength to walk in Your will and Your way so that I may reach my destiny. In Jesus' name I pray, Amen.

Notes:

_____
_____
_____
_____
_____
_____
_____
_____
_____
_____

Chapter 1
Surrender

IT IS TIME TO MOVE BEYOND ACCEPTING CHANGE TO EMBRACING TRANSFORMATION

Golden Nugget:
"...*nevertheless not my will, but thine, be done*" (Luke 22:42).

Surrender is probably the most difficult part of anyone's journey. Think about it. Most humans would rather live under the illusion of having control rather than face the truth of being powerless. Most people would rather spend their entire lives pretending they are in charge than admit they are subject to forces or circumstances beyond their control.

What is it about living with an illusion that seems to keep people "happy"? An illusion is something that deceives by producing a false or misleading impression of reality. We live in a world of deception. This is why we should honor and follow God's plan for our lives. He knows the deceit that lies within this world. He is the only one who can help us. But we must first surrender to His wisdom and to His will.

Satan is the master of deception and if we are not careful we will find ourselves surrendering to the will of satan rather than the will of God. To avoid evil trappings the Bible tells us to put on the whole armor of God. He also commands us to study to show ourselves "approved unto God, a workman that needeth not to be ashamed, rightly dividing the word of truth" *(2 Timothy 2:15)*.

The only way to successfully surrender to God is to learn who He is. So let us explore who God is and how we can begin to live a life of surrender.

Reflections:

Identify some Scriptures that describe who God is. Write them out completely.

_____
_____
_____
_____
_____
_____
_____
_____

Describe briefly how God has revealed Himself to you personally.

_____
_____
_____
_____
_____
_____
_____
_____

Surrender

Definition of Surrender:
The ability to completely relinquish your self-will, admit your powerlessness, and submit to God's purpose and plan for your life despite the cost.
What is your definition of surrender?

_____
_____
_____
_____
_____
_____

How does your definition of surrender align itself with the Word of God?

_____
_____
_____
_____
_____
_____
_____
_____
_____
_____

Have you COMPLETELY surrendered your life to God?
If yes, how do you know?

_____
_____
_____
_____
_____
_____
_____

If no, what areas of your life are not completely surrendered to God?

_____
_____
_____
_____
_____
_____
_____
_____
_____
_____

What is keeping you from COMPLETE surrender?

_____
_____
_____
_____
_____
_____
_____
_____

Action:

What one thing will you do today to learn more about who God is?

_____
_____

What one thing will you do differently this week as you move toward living a life of surrender?

_____
_____

Surrender

Prayer:

Lord, thank You for Your grace and Your mercy. I thank You in advance for revealing more of who You are to me each day. Thank You for giving me a deeper understanding of what it means to surrender to You and the plans You have for my life. Thank You for helping me see that half-hearted surrender is equivalent to no surrender. I ask You, Lord, to reign in my life. Take charge. I want You to permeate every part of me. I now know that true strength lies in my ability to lay down my will and embrace Yours. I now know that the purpose of surrender is so that I might gain life. Proof that I have totally surrendered my life to You is when I can trust You, Lord; and proof that I trust You is when I am obedient. In Your Son Jesus' name, Amen.

Notes:

Chapter 2
God's Perfect Will

MY THOUGHTS ARE NOT YOUR THOUGHTS, NOR ARE MY WAYS YOUR WAYS

Golden Nugget:
>"For I know the plans I have for you, declares the Lord, plans to prosper you and not to harm you, plans to give you hope and a future" (Jeremiah 29:11 NIV).

Most people have difficulty grasping the concept that God's desire for our lives is that we live perfect, whole and complete. They don't truly believe God's will is PERFECT because they only view perfection in the natural sense. Remember, "God is a Spirit: and they that worship him must worship him in spirit and in truth" *(John 4:24)*.

So those who struggle with the concept of perfection have not yet learned to worship God in spirit and in truth. Truly, nothing in this world will ever make sense until we understand that we are spiritual beings operating in a carnal body. Oftentimes we have difficulty identifying and walking in God's will for our lives because we allow the trappings of this world to dull our spiritual senses. It is important to sharpen and fine tune our spiritual senses daily. When we do this we will find ourselves in a place where we can hear from God more clearly.

God has a master plan. He is the ultimate architect. He is the master builder. Following His blueprint is the only way we will find success!

Reflections:

Have you identified God's perfect will for your life?
If yes, What is His will for your life?

_____
_____
_____
_____
_____
_____

How was it revealed to you?

_____
_____
_____
_____

Are you walking in your calling? Why or why not?

_____
_____
_____
_____
_____

God's Perfect Will

Give an example of a time you confused your will with God's will.

_____
_____
_____
_____
_____

Why do you think confusion set in?

_____
_____
_____
_____
_____

Have you ever allowed your emotions to cause you to doubt God? If yes, give an example:

_____
_____
_____
_____
_____
_____

What was the outcome?

_____
_____
_____
_____
_____

How could you have handled the situation differently?

_____
_____
_____
_____
_____
_____
_____
_____

What lesson(s) did you learn?

_____
_____
_____
_____
_____
_____
_____

Has your will (plan) ever gotten in the way of God's will (purpose) for your life?
If yes, give an example:

_____
_____
_____
_____
_____
_____
_____
_____

God's Perfect Will

What was the outcome?

How could you have handled the situation differently?

What lesson(s) did you learn?

What must you do to fall in line with God's perfect will?

_____
_____
_____
_____
_____
_____
_____
_____
_____
_____
_____
_____
_____
_____
_____
_____
_____
_____
_____
_____
_____
_____
_____
_____
_____

Action:

Find 3 scriptures in the Bible that will help you learn how to identify God's will for your life.

1. _____
2. _____
3. _____

God's Perfect Will

Prayer:

Lord, thank You for Your awesome knowledge, wisdom and foresight; for You know the end from the beginning. Help me to place full trust in You and Your perfect plan. For I know that once I learn to trust You completely I will experience less stress and anxiety. If I learn to trust Your perfect plan for my life I will experience peace even in the midst of the storm. Teach me to hear Your voice clearly so that I never confuse my will with Yours. I want Your will to be done in my life. I no longer want my will. My will has proven to be detrimental to my mind, body and soul. Your will has and always will bring peace and joy. I thank You in advance for leading me into truth and righteousness. In Jesus' name I pray, Amen.

Notes:

Chapter 3
God's Perfect Timing

REST IN THE LORD AND WAIT PATIENTLY FOR HIM

Golden Nugget:
> "To every thing there is a season, and a time to every purpose under the heaven" (Ecclesiastes 3:1).

Whether we believe it or not, there is power in waiting. Oftentimes we become restless. We become impatient and want things to happen *now*, almost as soon as the thought arises in our minds. Restlessness and impatience sometimes get in the way because we are not attuned to the Holy Spirit.

Becoming restless is also a sign that we want our way more than we want God's way. This is a fragile state to be in because when we become anxious and restless we are liable to make decisions that are outside the will of God. When we find ourselves feeling this way, we must remember God's Word, where He says, "But they that wait upon the Lord shall renew their strength; they shall mount up with wings as eagles; they shall run, and not be weary; and they shall walk, and not faint" *(Isaiah 40:31)*. Trusting is a major part of waiting. If we can trust God and take Him at His word we will experience less anxiety and stress.

Part of trusting God is acting on His word. As you have read in *Change Beyond The Pain*, working is also a major part of waiting. Waiting doesn't mean that we sit around and do nothing while God does everything. We must serve in the capacity to which He has called us until we see His will made manifest in our lives.

Reflections:

Since a major part of "waiting" is working, it is important to understand the season of your life you are in spiritually so that you will be better able to understand what "work" you should be doing.

Everything the farmer does is based on the principle of seasons~timing~purpose.

Identify a specific area in your life where you had a difficult time applying this principle. (Refer to Chapter 3 to refresh your memory about the farmer's principles.)

_____
_____
_____
_____

What was the outcome?
_____
_____
_____
_____

God's Perfect Timing

How could you have managed the situation differently?

_____
_____
_____
_____
_____
_____
_____

Seasons come and seasons go. Explore the four natural seasons and determine how they also relate to the spiritual seasons in your life.

What happens naturally during each season?
What happens spiritually during each season?
What does God's Word say about how we can endure/overcome each season?

Winter

Physical Characteristics: (i.e. it is extremely cold)

_____
_____
_____
_____
_____
_____

Spiritual Characteristics: (i.e. facing difficult trials)

_____
_____
_____
_____
_____
_____

Encouraging Scriptures: (i.e. *Hebrews 3:14*: "For we are made partakers of Christ, if we hold the beginning of our confidence steadfast unto the end.")

_____
_____
_____
_____
_____

Spring

Physical Characteristics:

_____
_____
_____
_____
_____

Spiritual Characteristics:

_____
_____
_____
_____
_____

Encouraging Scriptures:

_____
_____
_____
_____

Summer

Physical Characteristics:

_____
_____
_____
_____
_____

Spiritual Characteristics:

_____
_____
_____
_____
_____

Encouraging Scriptures:

_____
_____
_____
_____
_____

Fall

Physical Characteristics:

_____
_____
_____
_____
_____

Spiritual Characteristics:

_____
_____
_____
_____
_____

Encouraging Scriptures:

_____
_____
_____
_____
_____

Has God promised you something? If so, identify what He promised you.

_____
_____
_____
_____
_____

Identify what you will do while you are waiting for God's promise to come to pass.

_____
_____
_____
_____
_____

God's Perfect Timing

There are certain characteristics that must be considered and exercised in every season. However, we don't always take the time to explore these characteristics in depth, thus keeping us from truly progressing in our walk with Christ. Let us take a moment to explore what it really takes to move forward no matter what season you are in your life.

Courage
Definition: _____
_____

When do you feel the least courageous and why?
_____
_____
_____
_____
_____
_____
_____
_____

Hard work
Definition: _____
_____

What makes you resistant to hard work?
_____
_____
_____
_____
_____
_____
_____

Faith
Definition: _____
_____

What makes it hard for you to believe?
_____
_____
_____
_____
_____
_____

Endurance
Definition: _____
_____

What causes you to give up?
_____
_____
_____
_____
_____
_____

Pain
Definition: _____
_____

Why may you find it difficult to see value in your pain?
_____
_____
_____
_____

Consistency
Definition: _____
_____

What causes you to be inconsistent at times?
_____
_____
_____
_____
_____
_____
_____
_____
_____
_____

Timing
Definition: _____
_____

When it comes to following God's will, do you find yourself moving *before time*, *on time* or *late*?
_____
_____
_____
_____
_____
_____
_____
_____
_____
_____

Expectation
Definition: _____
_____

Why is it important to have an attitude of expectation regardless of what season of your life you find yourself in?

_____
_____
_____
_____
_____
_____
_____

Joy
Definition: _____
_____

What have you done to find joy during the difficult times in life?

_____
_____
_____
_____
_____
_____
_____

Action:
Have you been procrastinating? If so, what will you do today to break the cycle of procrastination so that you can begin to operate within God's divine timing?

_____
_____

Prayer:

Lord, thank You for being an awesome teacher and an awesome guide. There is none like You. Lord, please teach me how to wait. Teach me how to embrace every season of my life, knowing that there is growth and maturity in You no matter what is happening. Help me understand that moving in Your perfect timing is crucial. I must not operate in my flesh. When I hear a word from You, give me the courage and the strength to follow Your will completely just as You have instructed me to. Help me to embrace the fact that there is power in waiting; knowing that waiting ultimately means serving. Thank You in advance for guiding me and helping me to move in Your perfect timing. In Jesus' name I pray, Amen.

Notes:

Chapter 4
All For His Glory... It's Not About Me

KNOW YOUR ROLE IN THE KINGDOM OF GOD

Golden Nugget:
"*Thou art worthy, O Lord, to receive glory and honor and power: for thou hast created all things, and for thy pleasure they are and were created*" (Revelation 4:11).

Understanding the concept of God getting all the glory is probably one of the most fundamental principles we will need to embrace in order to begin the process of transformation. Knowing what God wants for us and from us is the key that will unlock the door to our freedom.

Learning how to move ourselves out of the way is vital to the process. We cannot be selfish and self-centered and expect to arrive at the destination God has called us to. We have to understand that this life is not about us. We must be willing and eager to do God's will but we must do it without impure motives. We must not seek praise, recognition, glory or exaltation. All of that belongs to God. When we accept this, completing the tasks He has for us becomes so much more rewarding.

Reflections:

Have you completely grasped the idea that this life is not about you? Whether the answer is yes or no, what facts helped you reach this conclusion?

_____
_____
_____
_____
_____
_____
_____
_____

Has selfishness or pride ever been part of your character on any level? If yes, how has it affected your life (or how is it currently affecting your life)?

_____
_____
_____
_____
_____
_____
_____
_____

All For His Glory... It's Not About Me

Is God's glory being seen in your life?
If yes, how?

_____
_____
_____
_____
_____
_____
_____

If no, in what ways are you blocking this?

_____
_____
_____
_____
_____
_____
_____

Action:

Today I will glorify God by:

1. _____
   _____

2. _____
   _____

3. _____
   _____

Prayer:

Lord, You are so awesome and there is no one above You. Your power and infinite wisdom simply amaze me. You alone are worthy to be praised. I am humbled You chose me to give You glory. Teach me my role within the Kingdom of God, so that I may operate effectively within Your will. Whenever I go through a trial, help me to see my situation simply as an opportunity for Your power and glory to shine through. Where there is pride, cast it down. Where there is lust, tear it away. Where there is selfishness, remove it from my life. Where there is envy, destroy it. Where there is deceit, replace it with truth. For this is the only way I can do Your will and bring glory and honor to You. In Jesus' name I pray, Amen.

Notes:

Chapter 5
The Power And Purpose Of Pain

Golden Nugget:
"...all things work together for good to them that love God, to them who are the called according to his purpose" (Romans 8:28).

Pain is a very important and necessary part of life. In the medical field, pain is defined as an unpleasant sensory and emotional experience associated with actual or potential tissue damage. Pain motivates us to withdraw from damaging situations, protects damaged body parts while they heal, and serves as a reminder to avoid similar situations in the future. Even though pain is extremely unpleasant, it has a profound purpose; a purpose other than to cause us discomfort and make our lives miserable. Knowing the purpose for our pain will make our painful experience worthwhile.

Pain often serves as a platform that elevates us to the next level. We have to learn how to identify the power and purpose in our pain. There are so many things that keep us stuck: fear, anger, rejection, hurt, etc. Most people, however, are unable to move to the next level because they do not recognize that power and purpose can be found in every situation that a child of God goes through. God does not waste an experience. Power and purpose can be found in all things He allows in our lives.

Reflections:

Do you truly believe there is power and purpose in pain?

a. If Yes, why?

_____
_____
_____
_____
_____
_____
_____
_____

b. If No, why not?

_____
_____
_____
_____
_____
_____
_____

The Power And Purpose Of Pain

Identify a situation that caused you significant pain (spiritual, physical or emotional).

_____
_____
_____
_____
_____
_____
_____
_____

Were you able to find purpose in your pain? If so, what was it?

_____
_____
_____
_____
_____
_____
_____
_____

Identify a person in the Bible whose story inspires you to keep moving forward despite whatever pain you may be experiencing.

_____
_____
_____
_____
_____
_____
_____

List the person's attributes and talk about why this person inspires you.
_____
_____
_____
_____
_____
_____
_____
_____
_____
_____

Identify a trial you successfully made it through and how you were able to help someone else make it through a similar situation.
_____
_____
_____
_____
_____
_____
_____
_____
_____
_____

Action:
Today, whenever a negative thought pops into your mind, replace it immediately with a positive thought.
Write Scripture verses and positive thoughts on sticky notes and place them in personal spaces that you frequent.

The Power And Purpose Of Pain

Prayer:

Lord, I will not allow the enemy to distort my vision. I know You have a plan for my life. I realize the enemy is here to kill my spirit, steal my joy and destroy the plans You have for my life. I also know that he is already defeated. Lord, show me how to use my test as a testimony to help someone else make it through their trial. Thank You for each and every obstacle You have allowed in my life. Thank You for teaching me that there is power and purpose in my pain. Father, I thank You for showing Yourself strong in my weakness. Thank You for forgiving all my sins, healing all my pain and mending my broken heart. I am excited and I can now move forward into my destiny because I know without a doubt there is power and purpose in my pain. In Jesus' name I pray, Amen.

Notes:

Chapter 6
Faith... But First You MUST Believe!

FAITH DOESN'T ASK QUESTIONS, IT SIMPLY FOLLOWS INSTRUCTIONS.

Golden Nugget:
   "*For we walk by faith, not by sight*" (2 Corinthians 5:7).

Faith doesn't ask questions, it simply follows instructions. The dictionary defines faith as a noun that means confidence or trust in something or someone. Furthermore, faith is a strong unshakeable belief in something without proof or evidence. While all this is true, I must go on record saying that in my eyes faith is not simply a noun. It is also a verb, an action word.

Faith is a spiritual term and operates in the spiritual realm. Faith does not operate under human logic. Faith is not based on the reasonableness of what God says, but simply on the fact that God said it. Faith does not require proof before something happens. Faith hears God speak and moves simply because the words came from the Lord.

***Reflections*:**

Remember, FAITH = MOVEMENT.
Describe a time when God gave you specific instructions and you did not follow through on the task.

_____
_____
_____
_____
_____
_____
_____
_____
_____
_____

Why didn't you follow through on the task?

_____
_____
_____
_____
_____
_____
_____
_____
_____

What were the consequences of your disobedience?

_____
_____
_____
_____
_____
_____
_____
_____

What lesson(s) did you learn?

_____
_____
_____
_____
_____
_____
_____
_____

What would you do differently next time and why?

_____
_____
_____
_____
_____
_____
_____
_____

Identify a Biblical story that is instrumental in helping you strengthen your faith in God.

___

Action:
Every day for the next week, locate and write down a Scripture in the Bible that will help you solidify your faith in God.

Prayer:

Father, You are awesome! Your word is powerful and true. Help me Lord, as I continue on my spiritual journey. Root up any seed of doubt, fear and confusion the enemy has planted. Replace it with clarity, confidence and courage. I now know that FAITH = MOVEMENT. When You speak, Lord, help me to move at the right time and the right way so that Your perfect will may be fulfilled. I understand I cannot operate out of my emotions; neither can I operate out of my own thinking, because Your word declares that Your thoughts and ways are not ours. I thank You in advance for ordering my steps and for increasing my faith. In Jesus' name I pray, Amen.

Notes:

Chapter 7
Transformation... It's An Inside Job!

DRILLING...BLASTING...REFINING

Golden Nugget:
"If we confess our sins, he is faithful and just to forgive us our sins, and to cleanse us from all unrighteousness" (1 John 1:9).

Transformation is an inside job. Although we may see evidence of transformation on the outside, it is the metamorphosis that takes place on the inside that makes the difference. Outside change is almost always temporary and is usually dictated by circumstances and outside influences. When real transformation takes place, there are very few things, if any, that will affect the metamorphosis that has occurred.

The butterfly is an amazing creature that provides us with a beautiful image of what the transformation process is like. This beautiful creature did not start off looking beautiful, however; it went through a process that is neither very pretty nor often talked about. The journey from lowly caterpillar to gorgeous butterfly is absolutely mesmerizing. If the butterfly could talk I am sure it would have quite a story to tell about its transformation process. Another thing I noticed about the butterfly's process is that no matter how much anyone admires its beauty, it had to go through the transformation process alone. We are like the butterfly. No matter how others admire our growth, we must undergo the transformation process on our own.

Reflections:

What revelation(s) has God given you about yourself?
_____
_____
_____
_____
_____

What has been your response to each revelation?
_____
_____
_____
_____
_____

What areas of your life has God drilled, blasted and refined?
_____
_____
_____
_____
_____

Action:
Look up the butterfly's transformation process and compare it to the process of your own spiritual life transformation.

Prayer:
Lord, I ask that You clean me up like only You can. Though my sins are as scarlet, I know You are the only one who can make me white as snow. Purity, love and honesty are what I desire. I now know that transformation is like surgery, and only the surgeon knows what procedures need to be done in order to make the patient whole again. You are my surgeon, Lord, and I give You permission to operate on me. I give You free reign over my life. I surrender all to You. Remove anything that is hindering my growth and progress in You. I am tired of making it seem as though everything is great when in actuality my life seems like a mess. I am ready for Your Spirit to clean me up and fill me. I want transformation to occur from the inside and I know it can only be found in You. In Jesus' name I pray, Amen.

Notes:

_____
_____
_____
_____
_____
_____
_____
_____
_____
_____
_____
_____
_____
_____

Chapter 8
Transformation Is Within Your Reach

Promotion Attained In The Heat Of The Night

Golden Nugget:
> "For promotion cometh neither from the east, nor from the west, nor from the south. But God is the judge: he putteth down one, and setteth up another" (Psalm 75:6-7).

Pain is often a catalyst for change. Going to the next level requires that we evaluate our thinking and become more aware of our vulnerabilities. We have to remember to look at our situations with our spiritual eyes. We have to look at pain differently. Oftentimes we view pain as an evil force, but pain can take us to the next level if we allow it.

We must remember that no matter what our circumstances look like, God is in control. He can turn the heart of the king in our favor should

He choose to do so. Many times transformation comes after we have gone through the fires of hardship and pain. That is when we need to remember that fire purifies. There is also something about the dark that brings clarity; something about the storms in our life seems to put things in perspective and cause us to look at life through a different lens. This new and different perspective is what takes us to the next level. So we cannot despise the process, for it is the process that promotes us.

Reflections:

List 5 areas of your life that need to be transformed and indicate why you need the transformation to take place.

_____
_____
_____
_____
_____
_____
_____
_____
_____
_____
_____
_____

Instead of looking at pain as something negative, let us view it as a positive force designed to catapult us to the next level. Having said that, let's talk about the following acronym for **P.A.I.N.** How would you define each stage? Are you ready for each stage?

Promotion
Definition: _____
_____
_____

What needs to take place in your life in order for you to be promoted (go to the next level) in Christ?

_____
_____
_____
_____
_____
_____
_____

Attained
Definition: _____
_____

After doing a serious self-inventory, are you honestly ready to attain what God has for you? Why or why not?

_____
_____
_____
_____
_____
_____
_____

In the heat of
Definition: _____
_____

How do you protect yourself (spiritually) when trials come in life?

_____
_____
_____
_____
_____
_____

Night
Definition: _____
_____

What fears do you have about the night?
_____
_____
_____
_____
_____
_____

How does the Word of God instruct you on how to combat those fears?
_____
_____
_____
_____
_____
_____

Write a prayer to God asking Him to transform your life.
_____
_____
_____
_____
_____
_____
_____
_____
_____

Action:

Today, start your day with Scripture, prayer and meditation. Meditate on that Scripture all week.

Prayer:

Lord, I thank You in advance for my promotion. Even when my way seems dark, I say thank You because I know You are with me. I thank You for the heat that is being turned up in my life because I know You are purifying me and getting me ready for promotion. I am so grateful that no weapon formed against me shall prosper. I am grateful that everything is working out for my good because I love You and You have called me for Your purpose. I will not despair, because my hope is in You. I will not distress. I will simply direct all my prayers and supplications toward You. In Jesus' name I pray, Amen.

Notes:

___
___
___
___
___
___
___
___
___
___
___
___
___
___
___

Change Beyond The Pain
Transformation Is Within Your Reach Workbook

By: Monifa Robinson Groover

Available for purchase online and in stores:
Amazon
Barnes & Noble
…and more!

Follow us on Facebook: Within Your Reach
Follow us on Twitter: @WYRInspires
Website: www.withinyourreach.org
Address: P.O. Box 60393
Savannah, GA 31420

Contact the author for interviews,
speaking engagements, retreats and more!

This workbook will teach you how to transform your life. Utilizing the strength of the Word of God and this guide as a tool, Change Beyond The Pain will empower you to gain a deeper understanding of what God is trying to impart in all of us.

The *Change Beyond The Pain Workbook* will help you discover:

- How true healing comes from allowing God to transform your life.
- How to stop repeating the same cycles of hurt, anger, fear and depression.
- That God has a plan for your life.
- There is power and purpose in your pain to help you experience positive and productive transformation.

You will learn how to move beyond accepting change to embracing transformation. So, if you are seeking restoration, read this book with an open heart, and together with your bible let the transformation begin.

Monifa Robinson Groover has been called by God and has devoted her life to helping others reach their God-given potential. Her experience has taught her that neither position nor status dictate the level of pain and misfortune one may encounter. Her duty is to equip others with the proper tools and resources to move beyond their circumstances and live healthier and more productive lives, which she believes can only be found when one has a relationship with Jesus Christ. Her personal journey, combined with her education and work experience, and most importantly, her relationship with Jesus Christ, collectively play a vital role in the work she passionately does today. She is a faithful member of New Covenant Holiness Church #3, located in Savannah, Georgia, where her beloved husband, Jamie Groover, is pastor.

$12.95
ISBN 978-0-9836776-2-8

www.ingramcontent.com/pod-product-compliance
Lightning Source LLC
Chambersburg PA
CBHW051957290426
44110CB00015B/2281